A Woman Of Worth:
Loving the Skin I'm In

Dr. Jacquelyn Hadnot

A Woman of Worth: Loving the Skin I'm In

©copyright 2012 Dr. Jacquelyn Hadnot

A Woman of Worth: Loving the Skin I'm In
Dr. Jacquelyn Hadnot
Published by: Igniting the Fire Publishing
1314 North 38th Street
Kansas City, KS 66102
www.ignitingthefire.net

No part of this publication may be reproduced, stored in a retrieval system, or transmitted, in any form or by any means, electronic, mechanical, photocopying, recording, or otherwise, without the written prior permission of the author.

Unless otherwise noted, all Scripture quotations are taken from King James Version of the Bible.

Scripture quotations marked AMP are taken from The Amplified Bible AMP. The Amplified Bible, Old Testament copyright © 1965, 1987 by the Zondervan Corporation. The Amplified New Testament, copyright © 1954, 1958, 1987 by the Lockman Foundation. Used by permission.

Scripture quotations marked NASB are taken from The New American Standard Bible AMP. Copyright © 1960, 1962, 1963, 1968, 1971, 1972, 1973, 1975, 1977 by the Zondervan Corporation. The Amplified New Testament, copyright © 1954, 1958, 1987 by the Lockman Foundation. Used by permission.

Scripture quotations marked NIV are taken from The New International Version. Copyright © 1973, 1978, 1984 by the International Bible Society. Used by permission.

Cover Design: Dr. Jacquelyn Hadnot
Copyright© 2012 by Dr. Jacquelyn Hadnot
All rights reserved.

Please note that Igniting the Fire's publishing style capitalizes certain pronouns in Scripture that refer to the Father, Son, and Holy Spirit, and may differ from some Bible publishers' styles.

Table of Contents

Introduction	7
1 What is Value?	13
2 To Value or Not to Devalue?	19
3 Two Enemies at Work	31
4 How Can I Dance If You Are on My Feet?	37
5 The Many Layers of a Woman	45
6 The Scent of a Woman	49
7 You Don't Know My Story	55
8 I Am Not a Rent-a-Cop	65
9 Has the Church Lowered the Bar?	79
10 Are You a Grasshopper in Your Own Eyes?	91
11 Even Rahab Had Value	97
12 A Woman of Inheritance	101
13 I'm Bad!	105
14 Loving the Skin I'm In	109
15 Love Yourself in the Process	115
16 Discovering the Butterfly in You	119
About the Author	129
Books By Dr. Jacquie	133
Contact Information	134
Journal	136

A Woman of Worth: Loving the Skin I'm In

Dedication

Apostle Ella Crawford for being an awesome woman of God and for allowing God to use you to push me into my destiny. That tap on the shoulder changed my life. Thank you for being obedient to the voice of the Lord.

Pastor Olivia C.Q. Aiken for being an inspiration to all women and for putting the final touch on the title of this book by simply speaking a word.
Your message resonated in my heart.

Pastor Valerie Thornton, Apostle Sarah White, Dr. Margaret Wright, Apostle Mary Gilbert, Evangelist Bernia Williams, and Lady Sandra Johnson, I love you all so very much.
Thanks for always encouraging me.

To the great women of God around the world standing firm on the frontlines for the Kingdom of God.

To the women that are discovering who they are and whose they are - step, my sisters, step.

A Woman of Worth: Loving the Skin I'm In

Introduction

There is something very special about a woman and her worth. Worth means the value of something. A woman's worth is priceless, it is worth more than money, fortune or fame. A woman is a rare jewel that is to be treasured because she is fearfully and wonderfully made by the hand of God.

From the beginning, women were fashioned in a way that her value was unmistakable. She was born from the rib of man, yet shaped in the image of the invisible God who created her. She was molded to be strong, yet fragile. Wise yet gentle. Humorous while at the same time serious. She was created with the ability to be versatile while maintaining the ability to be flexible in any situation. She was tailor made by God to do great exploits. She was endowed with the gifts of love, joy, self-control, peace, patience, gentleness, longsuffering, kindness, goodness and faithfulness. She was endowed with the gift of reproduction. She reproduces through her children, music, ministry, business, education and more. In other words, God created women to embody the fullness of the helpmate for man and the kingdom of God.

Why it is so easy for society to de-value the worth of a woman? Why is it so easy for a woman to be treated like a second-class citizen? How can society attempt to reduce a woman's worth to less than the price of a hamburger? While at the same time relying on her to have all the answers to life's little complexities? In the workplace, she is often paid less than a man, while being required to do twice as much work. When a woman is determined, she is labeled aggressive or controlling, while her male counterpart is motivated. On the other hand, the man is considered forceful and she is labeled with a four or five letter word.

I found myself asking these questions at a time when God began to reveal that I had allowed people and circumstances to devalue me as a person and as a woman of God.

I often refer to myself as "A woman after God's own heart." If that is the case, then how can I be less than fearfully and wonderfully made by the same God who created man?

How is it that I can allow a godless society to define or devalue me? How can I believe the lies and deceptions of the enemy? How can I allow anyone or anything to lessen my worth in the sight of Almighty God? What can society accomplish by devaluing women?

I pray that as I put pen to paper, together we will find the answers to every question that has perplexed us on this sensitive subject.

It is not my intent to *man bash*, *people bash* or even *church bash*. My intent is to expose one of the most horrendous lies ever perpetrated against women. What is the lie? Women are of little or lesser value.

So begins our journey together - a journey to discover a woman's worth or value. I pray that at the end of this book you will find the strength within yourself to address any issues that have plagued you or hindered your purpose and

A Woman of Worth: Loving the Skin I'm In

destiny. I believe that by the time you reach the end of this book you will know without a doubt that you are a woman of worth.

A Woman of Worth: Loving the Skin I'm In

Chapter 1

What is Value?

Let's establish an understanding of the terms, value and devalue. It is vital to have a good understanding of each word if we are to search our hearts to determine if we are walking in the realm of devaluation.

Webster defines **value** as:
- ✓ The quality of a thing according to which it is thought of being more or less desirable, useful, estimable, important.
- ✓ That which is desirable or worthy of esteem for its own sake.

A Woman of Worth: Loving the Skin I'm In

- ✓ Thing or quality having intrinsic worth.
- ✓ To place a certain estimate of worth on a scale of values.

What does the term **worth** mean?
- ✓ The esteem in which a person or thing is held.
- ✓ Importance, value, merit, excellence.

What does it mean to **devalue**?
- ✓ To make or become less valuable.
- ✓ To cause the value or importance of somebody or something to be reduced.
- ✓ To become reduced in value or importance.

The terms **worth** and **value** are used interchangeably when applied to the interest of something. Worth also implies a fundamental excellence resulting from higher moral, cultural or spiritual qualities, and value suggests the excellence accredited to something with reference to its usefulness or significance.

I pray that the definitions help to define the terms we will be addressing throughout our journey. In all our getting, let's make sure we get an understanding. Why? People are destroyed because they lack the knowledge needed for change or growth.

The day the Lord revealed that I had allowed myself to be devalued, was the day that I had to search my heart, my mind, my life and everyone and everything around me to determine how and why I allowed it to creep in. "And that because of false brethren unawares brought in, who came in privily to spy out our liberty which we have in Christ Jesus, that they might bring us into *bondage*" (Galatians 2:4 italics added).

I like Galatians 2:4 because it describes how the

bondage of devaluation can so easily creep in. We are not going to reduce our own self-worth. It is slowly insinuated by the people and circumstances around us. The enemy realizes the freedom we walk in and fashions a trap to destroy the liberty that enables us to walk in the fullness of God.

> **Value is the quality of a thing according to which it is thought of being more or less desirable, useful, estimable, important.**

Throughout this book, I will share some of the traps set by the enemy and God's warnings to me regarding my journey of destroying the spirit of devaluation. I call it a spirit because it is not someone or something you can see, smell, taste or touch. It is a trap or snare of the enemy that is slow and methodical. Its sole purpose is to shut you down and cause you to stop believing in yourself. It also seeks to render you useless for the Kingdom of God and it hinders your ministry to those that are waiting for your God ordained destiny.

So begins my testimony and your freedom from another trap of the enemy - devaluation.

A Woman of Worth: Loving the Skin I'm In

Chapter 2

To Value or Devalue? That is the?

The enemy started his campaign against me the day I birthed my first music CD. Because I was new to the music industry, I had a wide eyed faith that the first CD was going to sell millions, bless me financially and give me the financial freedom to move into ministry full time. The fact that my gift is the "spoken word" did not deter me. I thought that since God spoke it, He had the final word and it was going to be the tool that changed my life. My feelings were battered and bruised during the first few years.

A Woman of Worth: Loving the Skin I'm In

Undaunted by the sales of the CD His Mercy Endures Forever, I set out on the ardent task of birthing CD number two, which was also a spoken word CD accomplished with the help of vocalists and producers of the highest caliber. Again sales were decent, but not what I expected. Finally, I birthed music CD number three and for the first year after its release, I didn't promote it AT ALL. I had become so disappointed with the sales of the first two CD's that I believed the lie of the enemy that no one wanted to hear the music. I bought into the lie to the extent that I allowed the music to sit on a shelf and went so far as to give CDs away whenever the opportunity presented itself.

While I was birthing music, I was also writing books. From 2006 to date, I have written approximately twenty-plus books and teaching manuals. At one point, I had five unpublished books sitting on my computer. Why? I believed the lie that no one wanted to hear what was inside me.

Writing for me is like a river that flows. I love to express my thoughts on paper. I enjoy the freedom I experience when I write. Words flow from my belly as clouds float across the sky.

Unfortunately, along the way I allowed the lies of the enemy and individuals strategically placed in my life to hinder the move of God and cause the spirit of devaluation to set in. Don't misunderstand, my books and CD's sold, in fact I received numerous music and book awards, but through the eyes of the enemy, it was not good enough.

People that I thought would be in my corner,

began to disappear and speak unkindly of me. As a person that strives to love unconditionally, it hurt and it hurt deeply. Within the hurt, I withdrew from ministering music publicly for a while and the process to devalue me continued at a slow and methodical pace.

> **The assignment to devalue your gifts will not bombard you; it will be slow and subtle.**

The assignment to devalue your gifts will not bombard you; it will be slow and subtle. It is not designed to pounce on you like a ravenous wolf; instead, it comes in very quietly and often goes unnoticed. Remember it is designed to stop the flow of God in and through your life.

I recall one evening in prayer the Lord spoke these words, "You have allowed people around you to devalue what I have put in you. You have stopped believing in yourself and therefore you are not moving forward."

Can you say "OUCH?" That hurt, but it was true. The hurt ran so deeply that I stopped ministering the music when I went to speak. The psalmist anointing on my life has always been my life's blood and the tool God used for my physical healing. For years, God's healing for His people flowed through the Psalmist anointing. The day I stopped believing in the music was the day that the flow of His healing power stopped flowing through me. It was a slow and systematic shutdown of power - God's power.

**Let's take a rabbit trail**: if you have read any of my books, you realize by now that every book

contains elements of a work that God has done through me. Some day He might allow me to write a romance novel, but in the meantime, I will continue to write about my life's experiences. I am an over comer by the blood of the lamb and by the very words of my testimony.

I allowed the enemy to stop God's flow because I stopped believing in the power of God flowing through me. I wanted the books and music to be accepted by people and their way of acceptance was by purchasing them. Face it, every artist, author, artisan or minister wants to be accepted for the work they have done.

To make matters worse, when I traveled to minister I no longer carried books or CD's with me. At that point, it seemed useless to take materials that I thought nobody wanted. Please know that those were the words of the enemy, but I bought the lie. The enemy set the trap to tear me down through devaluing everything in my life. As a minister of the gospel of Jesus Christ, we don't need confidence in ourselves; we must have confidence in the ONE that sends us out. Nevertheless, by that same token we must believe in the Christ that lives in us - if we are to go forth in **His** strength and power.

The best dreams in the world will mean nothing if you don't believe in them. The best business in the world will fail if you don't believe in it. The best marriage in the world will flounder if you don't love and nurture it.

Devaluation is a spiritually and emotionally invasive tactic of the enemy. Invasive because it attacks the very fiber of your mind and spirit, systematically shutting down your faith.

Because I believed the lies of the enemy, it caused the value or importance of the ministry inside me to be reduced. My books, CDs and teachings became less valuable to me. It went so far as to invade the preached word inside my belly. I found myself doubting the word I was preaching. I did not doubt the word of God, I doubted the messenger of the word - I doubted me.

 **Rabbit Trail**: I pray that this book helps you to see just how invasive the tactics of the enemy are. Don't judge the raw truth until you have been bitten by it. This is my raw truth and as transparent as I am, I am equally aware that some of you reading

this book might ask, how can she doubt and still call herself a woman of God. Keep living baby, if your day hasn't come - it will. The more you press for advancement, the more the enemy will launch attacks against you. Doubt then gives way to fear and the cycle continues.

Recently, I published a book entitled, "Closing the Doors to Satan's Attacks: Overcoming Fear." In it, I took the reader on my journey of overcoming fear. What I did not discuss in the book were the elements of devaluation that crept in while I was dealing with fear. I must have saved it for this book, truly a story within itself.

As you go through life, you will always encounter traps in your spiritual warfare battle. That is why I believe it is vital to be armed and ready to stand against the wiles of the devil.

"(For the weapons of our warfare are not carnal, but mighty through God to the pulling down of strong holds;) Casting down imaginations, and every high thing that exalteth itself against the knowledge of God, and bringing into captivity every thought to the obedience of Christ (2 Corinthians 10:4 -5)."

When we are devalued, it is important to realize that the attack begins in the mind. An imagination that:

- ✓ Tries to set itself against the knowledge of Christ that lives in you.
- ✓ Tries to destroy the knowledge that you are fearfully and wonderfully made in God's image.
- ✓ Tries to set itself against the fact that every good and perfect gift comes from above.

- ✓ Tries to destroy the fact that Jesus came so that you would have an abundant life.
- ✓ Is assigned to destroy the knowledge that Jesus commissioned us to "go ye into all nations" spreading the Good News of the gospel.

If we don't take the thoughts and imaginations of the enemy captive, they will take us captive and put us in bondage, rendering us useless vessels not fit or ready for the master's use. *"If a man therefore purge himself from these, he shall be a vessel unto honour, sanctified, and meet for the master's use, and prepared unto every good work"* (2 Timothy 2:21).

We must be purged from thoughts and feelings of worthlessness if we are to be useful for the Kingdom Agenda that is set before us. Purging requires that we dig through the many layers that make us women and men of God (Although this book is addressed to women, I believe men can benefit also. So share it with our brothers).

Chapter 3

Two Enemies at Work Behind Devaluation

There are two spirits in operation behind the scenes of devaluation. You must recognize them the moment they raise their diabolical heads. They are twins and they are deadly. Every time a negative word or action insinuates its ugly tentacle against you, two spirits are lurking behind the scenes to trap and manipulate you into succumbing to its deadly sting. What are the two spirits operating against you? Insecurity and inferiority.

The word *insecurity* means "the state of being unsafe, insecure or a state of mind characterized by self-doubt and vulnerability.

The word *inferiority* means lower or low in rank, standing, or degree, lower in quality or value mediocre: failing to meet a standard of quality, ability, or achievement.

Therefore, the spirit of devaluation causes an individual to feel unsafe and insecure. Thereby opening the door to inferiority because feelings of a lower value or quality have taken root.

Once feelings of devaluation have taken root, a door is opened for the spirits of insecurity and inferiority to have access and the attack begins. An attack with the ultimate goal of enslaving and shutting down the flow of God in the life of the individual. Unfortunately, other spirits now have

A Woman of Worth: Loving the Skin I'm In

an access point from which to gain entry into the life of the believer. See the listing below of other spirits that now have a legal right to come against you.

Self-Life Issues	**Description**
Anger	a strong feeling of grievance and displeasure
Arrogant	proudly contemptuous: feeling or showing self-importance & contempt or disregard for others
Bitterness	angry and resentful: expressing intense hostility
Boastful	overemphasize possessions or accomplishments: refer immodestly to possessions or achievements
Fear	unpleasant feeling of anxiety or apprehension
Hatred	intense, hostile intentions and acts; extreme dislike or enmity
Narcissism	self-absorption, conceit, vanity
Pride	arrogance, conceit, smugness, self-importance
Resentment	ill feeling: aggrieved feelings caused by a sense of having been badly treated
Self-disgust	self-loathing, self-disgust, self-dislike
Self-esteem	(LOW) lack of confidence in your own merit as an individual person
Self-doubt	lack of self-confidence: feelings of doubt about your own worth and abilities

A Woman of Worth: Loving the Skin I'm In

Self-hatred	self-contempt, self-loathing, self-disgust, self-denigration, self-dislike, self-abasement
Self-loathing	intense dislike of yourself
Self-pity	pity felt for self: self-indulgent belief that your life is harder & sadder than everyone else's
Unforgiveness	unwilling or unable to forgive
Vanity	excessive pride, especially in personal appearance
Worthlessness	having no good, attractive, or admirable qualities at all

This is a partial list of subordinate spirits that have a legal right to come against you when you are walking in insecurity and inferiority.

Devaluation is a deadly enemy and its only mission is to destroy your confidence in your worth. Once God begins to peel back the layers of insecurity and inferiority, He can begin to heal the wounds that lie beneath. God desires that we are whole, spiritually and mentally. He wants us ready to do a great work for the Kingdom. When the layers of pain and all the fragments and debris are removed and swept away, He can begin the process of discovering the many layers of a woman.

For a complete listing of self-life issues, check out my book, *The Enemy in Me: Overcoming Self-Life Issues.*

A Woman of Worth: Loving the Skin I'm In

Chapter 4

How Can I Dance When You're Standing on My Feet?

I love to dance because dancing is a form of praise, release, freedom and in some instances flight. Imagine when you were a child and you danced on the feet of your earthly father. You held on tight as he danced you around the room. With a giggle and wide-eyed smile, it almost felt like flying. There was freedom in the dance as you twirled around the room. As you grew into a teenager and went to parties and other affairs, if you were like me you would dance, with or without a partner because dancing was your outlet.

Fast forward to the place you are now and ask yourself, "do I still enjoy dancing?" My husband and I will dance around the family room to whatever music is playing because it is a form of togetherness and it brings us joy and laughter. Whether I am dancing with Gregg or alone - I love to dance.

During my season of going through the valley of devaluation, I found myself asking the question, how can I dance if you are standing on my feet? How can you dance with the freedom of an eagle if someone is standing on your feet? Unlike, the little girl who stood on her father's feet and danced, you are incapable of moving in the spirit when your spiritual feet are in bondage, weighed down with the cares of the world.

A Woman of Worth: Loving the Skin I'm In

When Satan is standing on your feet, how can you dance? When fear, doubt or insecurity sits on your heart like a ton of bricks, how can you dance? When the world has placed a low jack on your self-worth, how can you dance? When everyone around you tells you that you will never amount to anything, how can you dance? When the people in your inner circle turn their backs on you, and scandalize your name, how can you dance? When the people you placed in leadership positions in the church lie, connive and split the church, how can you dance? When the husband you love, trusted and believed in devalues the marriage and blames you for it, how can you dance?

Well, my dear sister when any scenario happens, dancing just might be the only thing you have left to hold on to. It may sound strange, but the enemy has designed your downfall by trying to take away your ability to dance. He wants you to retreat into a little corner and cower like a weak, pitiful little girl with no power or authority. He wants you to kick off your dancing shoes, throw them in the trash and stomp off defeated, bruised and rejected. Moreover, there may be days when that's how you feel, but that's not who you are. There may also be days, when you just don't feel like being anything, except left alone.

As a woman who has been in that dark lonely place, I can tell you that it's because you just don't have the strength to dance. The day I almost lost my strength to dance was the day that the enemy THOUGHT I was defeated. OH! The devil is a liar. Yes, I was down and retreated for a season. Yes, I thought my days of writing and birthing music were over and yes, I thought about getting a job and leaving ministry behind. BUT GOD! You can hide from many things and many people, but you cannot hide from God. It doesn't matter who is trying to kill your destiny, it is IMPOSSIBLE for them to kill something they did not give you in the first place. No man or woman on the face of the earth can stop your destiny because it is not in their weak manipulative power to accomplish such a great feat. They may hinder you for a while, they may even convince you to walk away for a season, but the destiny inside of you will not allow it, because greater is He that is in you than he that is in the world. Destiny and greatness are waiting to be birthed out of your spiritual belly.

Sometimes the "he" that is in the world might be your mother, father, sister, brother, husband or best friend. Watch out for the "he" that is trying to kill your seed by assassinating your ministry, character, destiny or self-worth.

> **Destiny and greatness are waiting to be birthed out of your spiritual belly.**

Spiritual assassins are ready to shoot your legs right out from under you. Yes, I said spiritual assassins who might be sitting in the cubicle next to you. Whispering in your ear during lunch, shopping with you, spending your money and trying to cut off your spiritual legs at the same time. Spiritual assassins will try to cut the baby right out of your belly, leaving you empty and bloody. You must recognize what is operating against you. The "what" is not a flesh and blood enemy, it is Satan and his diabolical hosts from hell. They are assigned to steal, kill and destroy you. If Satan can kill your joy, he can steal your peace. If he can steal your peace, he can destroy your faith. If he can destroy your faith, you are dead to the plans and purposes of God. (Read Second Corinthians 10:4-5, Ephesians 6:10-18).

As a woman of worth and spiritual warrior, you must recognize the spies trying to infiltrate the camp. You must pull down every stronghold and imagination that tries to exalt itself against what you know to be true about your God and your destiny.

If you haven't danced in a while, put on some praise music and dance. Simply, dance. If you enjoy walking, cut a little strut while you are walking. STAND on the feet of your Heavenly Father and dance my dear sister, DANCE!

A Woman of Worth: Loving the Skin I'm In

Chapter 5

The Many Layers of a Woman

Women come in many shapes, forms and sizes - tall, short, thin or thick madams. We come in every race, color and creed. No two women are alike. We are unique to the divine design of God because He fearfully and wonderfully made us.

Like a river, our layers run deep, like a river, we are constantly flowing in a deep vein called life. Moreover, like a river we can shift with the tides of life.

Our inner beauty can be as captivating as our

physical beauty. Armed with the mind and heart of God, we are unmovable, unshakable, and ready to stand our ground and war in the natural and in the spiritual realm. We are mighty through God ready to pull down strongholds and cast down every imagination that exalts itself against the knowledge of God and His purpose for our lives (2 Corinthians 10: 4-5 paraphrased).

Women are strong, fragile, and fearless while at the same time fearful. We can hold our own in the boardroom and yet be submissive in the bedroom. Women are tenacious yet flexible. No matter the situation, a woman is adaptable. Why? A woman with her many layers and nuances is comfortable in the skin she lives in. We are created with the "spirit of excellence" of the Lord. God created women to fulfill a work on the earth. Work that requires strength, humility, passion, compassion, obedience, trust and faith - faith in God and faith in ourselves. We were not created to simply walk around bare foot and pregnant. We were not created to serve and never be served. We were created to be celebrated and not simply tolerated.

> **Women are strong, fragile, and fearless while at the same time fearful. We can hold our own in the boardroom and yet be submissive in the bedroom.**

With the many layers of a woman, it is no wonder we have accomplished so much down through the years. We flow in many areas today that were once forbidden or taboo. Because of our ability to adapt to any situation, we can flow in places, spheres and realms that are often difficult for men. Please understand, I am not minimizing our husbands or brothers, I am simply stating that we are able to adapt to any situation. Our wombs were designed by God to adapt and give birth. Try pushing out a ten pound big head baby and see what I mean.

Because we are layered in the strength of the Lord, we have the ability and strength to endure trials, tribulations, hardships and pain. "How beautiful your sandaled feet, O prince's daughter" (Song of Songs 7:1)! We walk in a level of authority given to us by God. Our feet were created to stand in high heels or combat boots. We are comfortable walking in whatever shoes the situation demands. Why? Because we are steppers for the Kingdom of God.

Chapter 6

The Scent of a Woman

A woman's fragrance is unique, her very own. I am not talking about the scent from perfumes or colognes. I am talking about the very essence of a women's heart. A fragrance that enables her to be confident in her ability to stand and withstand. A fragrance that speaks to her strength, perseverance and determination.

Although the world would classify a woman as weak, timid and insecure - it is quite the opposite. By divine nature, we are caretakers, sustainers, nurturers. Our strength is often found in the areas that others deem weak. Our strengths are sometimes hidden behind the veil of devaluation.

As women, we are often belittled because of our ability to be strong yet silent, powerful while at the same time remain humble. A woman can walk **in** authority while at the same time submit **to** authority.

I believe that because women are strong in many areas, it makes them vulnerable in our lesser areas. That might be the reason many women end up in abusive relationships or settling for less than God's best. If we are not prayerful and watchful, our areas of vulnerability can be used against us. It is up to us to watch, pray, and allow the Lord to guide us in every area.

A woman is by nature a nurturer of those around her. The nurturer in her says, "Even though you don't appreciate me, I still love you and will care for you and I won't hold it against you." A woman's strength lies in her ability to love regardless of the pain she has endured over the years. Her skin is thick, yet tender. Her heart is strong yet easily broken.

> **When a woman finds the inner strength to embrace the beautiful scent God has blessed her with, her life and the lives of those around her will be enriched.**

The scent of a woman is all her very own. Our scent is not to be shared with everyone. A woman can walk into a room and change the atmosphere with a simple smile. The scent of a woman says, "I am a lady in the streets and a stone cold stepper in the sheets." Sheets that a woman of worth only shares with the man she has pledged her life to. The man she took vows

A Woman of Worth: Loving the Skin I'm In

to love, honor and obey. A woman of worth knows that a man will not buy the cow when he can get the milk for free. Therefore, she will not settle for warm thighs between satin sheets just to say she has a man. She knows that she is a treasure beyond price. A woman of worth knows that her scent is like a sweet bouquet; therefore, she would never allow anyone to cheapen her fragrance like that of a cheap dime store perfume.

When a woman finds the inner strength to embrace the beautiful scent God has blessed her with, her life and the lives of those around her will be enriched. When a woman is flowing at 100% everything around her flows with a great expectancy for growth and change. The old becomes the new. The impossible becomes the possible. The mediocre becomes excellent. The mundane becomes exciting. The scent of a

A Woman of Worth: Loving the Skin I'm In

woman changes everything around her because she is more than a pretty face; she is an agent of and for change in everything and everyone around her. The scent of woman tells her story…

A Woman of Worth: Loving the Skin I'm In

Chapter 7

You Don't Know My Story...

Over the years, I had met women that have overcome insurmountable odds to become women of purpose and destiny.

I am going to share some of their stories. I pray they will encourage, inspire and motivate you. Each woman has her own unique story, individual scars and personal triumphs. They are over comers by the blood of the lamb and by the very words of their testimonies.

A Woman of Worth: Loving the Skin I'm In

Valarie

Valerie is a pastor and teacher in a denomination dominated by men. During her pastoral assignment in her first church, she faced opposition from family members, church administration and even the congregation. Her passion for God kept her unmovable in her journey through ministry. She has been counted as weak because of her gentle but firm leadership skills. After years of coming under fire in the small church, God elevated her ministry to a larger church with more responsibilities because of her ability to stand and withstand.

The place where God has seated Valerie is in a seat of authority. She overcame every obstacle that was placed before her, and *she loves the skin she's in.*

Sandy

Sandy is a soft-spoken woman. She walks in a gentle authority that few recognize. Often misunderstood as weak and fearful, she is a woman that has a tender heart for God and His people. After living in the shadows of her husband, she has begun to walk in her purpose and destiny with the same quiet strength and determination she has carried for years. Her newly revealed strength in ministry and leadership has been a shock to many who know her, but undaunted she is determined to walk out the destiny God has placed before her. She is finding a new level of intimacy with the Lord and it is taking her to depths she never thought possible. In a new place of worship, *she loves the skin she's in.*

A Woman of Worth: Loving the Skin I'm In

Janice:

Janice is a woman of a destiny and legacy. She overcame a life of drugs, poverty, abuse and homelessness. She tells her story of drug addiction with honesty and openness. The tragic circumstances of abuse left her with emotional scars that have taken years to tear down. She spent over twenty years on drugs such as crack cocaine, cocaine, heroin and the like. Finally, she was determined to come face to face with her life and make a change. Change is exactly what she did. Today Janice is the epitome of an over comer. She is drug free, working in ministry full time, writing books and a living testimony to the power of God to set free and deliver those who have a desire for freedom. Her walk is straight, her stand is strong, and *she loves the skin she's in.*

A Woman of Worth: Loving the Skin I'm In

Bernia:

Who would have thought that a former drug addict, prostitute, madam and inmate could become a woman of purpose and destiny? Shunned by some, ostracized by others, this woman of strength decided that she would not allow others to dictate her destiny. The days of turning tricks for drugs are over and she is walking out her life with passion and purpose. She has birthed a ministry designed to encourage, inspire and motivate women to reach beyond their situation and walk into their destiny. In spite of her past, Bernia has grown into the woman that God predestined her to be. In fact, her past has made her stronger, more determined and inspired to reach as many hurting women as God will allow. Bernia is a woman of purpose and *she loves the skin she's in.*

A Woman of Worth: Loving the Skin I'm In

Carol:

Carol is a pastor's wife and mother who dedicated her life to family and ministry. Her husband, a man who carried a spirit of jealousy against her often held her back from walking in her purpose and destiny. Because of his insecurities, he resigned his pastorate and left the church in her care. After being gone for several months, he returned and placed a new pastor in position. The new pastor and trustees removed Carol from all leadership positions and informed her she was no longer needed. She left and pledged her membership to a new church.

Carol decided to sit for a season and discover the woman God created her to be. While she is on her journey *she's learning to love the skin, she's in.*

A Woman of Worth: Loving the Skin I'm In

Elmarie:

Elmarie shared her story one afternoon over lunch. For years, Pastor E walked in the power of God on her life and ministry. Unfortunately, individuals were strategically planted to try to shut down the flow of God in her ministry. One evening while complaining about the missiles the enemy had launched against her, the Lord informed her that she was complaining. He also said that she had allowed the enemy to devalue the calling on her life. The words of the Lord inspired a chapter in this book. The Lord asked, "Are you a grasshopper in your own eyes?" Words that changed her perspective forever.

God's loving correction brought Elmarie to a place where she accepts who she is and she *loves the skin she's in.*

A Woman of Worth: Loving the Skin I'm In

Sarah:

Sarah is a woman of many colors, layers and textures. She is a woman that is often misunderstood because of the uninhibited way she ministers. She is a woman that is confident, disciplined and dynamic. She is often avoided because of her outspoken ministry style. Her strong prophetic voice makes some people back away, partly because they are afraid she will see their hidden sins. She pulls no punches, speaks her mind and it is up to you to accept it. She is fair and impartial, only speaking the word of the Lord.

Sarah has found comfort in the close-knit circle of friends that love and accept her for who she is. She is a woman of worth and *she loves the skin she's in.*

A Woman of Worth: Loving the Skin I'm In

These women share several similarities:
- They are called to do a work for the kingdom.
- They have survived insurmountable obstacles.
- They are strong and determined.
- They have each been underestimated.
- They have each been devalued.
- They have found their purpose and destiny.
- They love the skin they are in.

We have all traveled different roads to become who we are. Everyone woman has a story to tell and each story is unique in its own way. No two stories are the same. There will be similarities but the stories, like the roads are different. Because our stories are different, we have the ability to minister to each other in many areas. Once we accept our differences, we can embrace our similarities.

A Woman of Worth: Loving the Skin I'm In

Never judge a woman by her outward appearance, beauty on the outside could mean ugliness on the inside. An outward plain Jane could be a beautiful butterfly inside.

We are fearfully and wonderfully made and that means that we are created with a beauty that cannot be duplicated. The inner beauty of a woman comes without a price - it cannot be bought or sold.

Once you hear the stories of the women in your life, you might be surprised to find that the jewel you have been searching for was right in front of you.

Chapter 8

I am NOT a Rent-A-Cop

It is my turn to share my journey through the valley of devaluation. If you have read any of my books or met me, you will know that I am anything but a weak woman. I am often defined as soft spoken because my voice is deep yet soft in volume. I am more of a teacher than a preacher of the word of God. I am also a Prophet of God who will stand flat-footed and proclaim the Word of God without the pomp and hype of more dynamic exhorters of the Word. To say that I am quiet in the presence of people I meet for the first time would be an accurate assessment. Because I am often quiet and soft-spoken, people sometimes get the impression that I am weak and powerless. They assume that I don't walk in the power and authority given to me by Christ Jesus.

Living in Kansas City has often been a challenge because individuals in the area have a tendency to put me in a neat little box and group me with other people in ministry. I find it interesting that in the business world I am viewed as strong, determined and one of the top accountants in the financial arena. Commanding as much as $150.00 to $175.00 per hour for consultation services. When I retired from the corporate world, my client base was in excess of 500 clients. As an accountant, I worked with budgets ranging in the millions. When it came to the financial arena I was strong and confident in my abilities.

A Woman of Worth: Loving the Skin I'm In

However, when it came to ministry, people wanted to put me in a box that read, she is simply a woman operating a food bank that feeds the needy. She is a local music artist with three or four CD's under her belt. Here is the ironic part: in Kansas City, I am considered a local artist or minister, but by national or international standards, my music and sermons have been heard in over 50 countries and 80 cities in the United States.

Their opinion does not affect me because I know who I am and whose I am. I find it sad that the people around me do not realize the power and favor of God that flows through me. "A prophet has no honor in his own country" (John 4:44).

Recently, I had an encounter with someone I will call Ted. For months, I maintained that Ted did not acknowledge the power of God flowing through my life. In other words, he did not take me serious in terms of the ministry or the anointing on my life.

What is the difference between a cop and a rent-a-cop? A police officer (cop) has authority to exercise the power that the judicial system gives him. A rent-a-cop has power limited to the building or area he is securing. A rent-a-cop has no authority when it comes to adjudicating the law.

Unfortunately, my friend viewed me as a rent-a-cop, someone who had no power or authority in the spirit realm. Someone who operated a ministry, walked in the office of Apostle, but carried no power or spiritual weight. His perspective of me was so low that when the Lord mandated that I give him a prophetic word, he did not receive it. He dismissed the Word from the Lord, but attempted to pacify me by pretending to acknowledge the message.

It is dangerous to deny the Word of the Lord simply because you do not value the messenger. Blood will be required at someone's hand. *"When I say to the wicked, 'You will surely die,' and you do not warn him or speak out to warn the wicked from his wicked way that he may live, that wicked man shall die in his iniquity, but his blood I will require at your hand. "Yet if you have warned the wicked and he does not turn from his wickedness or from his wicked way, he shall die in his iniquity; but you have delivered yourself. "Again, when a righteous man turns away from his righteousness and commits iniquity, and I place an obstacle before him, he will die; since you have not warned him, he shall die in his sin, and his righteous deeds which he has done shall not be remembered; but his blood I will require at your hand. "However, if you have warned the righteous man that the righteous should not sin and he does not sin, he shall surely live because he took warning; and you have delivered yourself"* (Ezekiel 3:18-21).

When God revealed to Ted his perspective of me it changed his entire mind set. I believe that he had devalued my authority in the spirit and earth realm for so long that it was commonplace for him to dismiss anything I offered. He did not accept me as a Prophet of God nor as a woman of God who walked in the power and authority of the God.

It's sad because for months he missed the

impartations that the Lord was trying to give him through me. He missed impartations in the areas of business and finances. I don't count it against him; I think it is sad because people often miss the spiritual depths of who we are because they are preoccupied with the external view of who we are. Unless you are loud and boisterous, you are viewed as weak and powerless. This type of mindset will cause us to miss the still quiet voice in which the Lord often speaks. The Lord is not screaming from the mountaintop, He is often in the whisper of the wind.

While we are waiting for the loud, clanging cymbals, the voice of the Lord is speaking in a place and manner that few will hear because they have not turned their spiritual ear to His frequency.

The spiritual frequency of the Lord is fine-tuned to the ear of those who are in a place of intimacy, prayer, fasting and consecration. Preaching, singing or being busy in ministry does not mean that we are in a place to hear the voice of the Lord.

> ***"The sacrifices of God are a broken spirit; A broken and a contrite heart, O God, You will not despise" (Psalm 51:17).***

I love my friend, but it saddened me to know that he did not value me as a woman of God. The truly sad part was that he was around me on a regular basis, while in reality I meant nothing to him in the realm of the spirit.

When God is ready to reveal His purpose, plan or people, he will do it in a way that you know without a doubt that it is God. He will use the very person, place or thing that you devalued to bring you to a place of humility. This is exactly what the Lord did with my friend. He used the very message I was mandated to deliver to bring him to a place of humility. Because the Lord was ready to move on his behalf and He could not move until a breaking occurred. "The sacrifices of God are a broken spirit; A broken and a contrite heart, O God, You will not despise" (Psalm 51:17). "For thus says the high and exalted One Who lives forever, whose name is Holy, "I dwell on a high and holy place, And also with the contrite and lowly of spirit In order to revive the spirit of the lowly And to revive the heart of the contrite" (Isaiah 57:15).

Repentance came the day the Lord showed my friend God's Eye View of me in a dream. In the dream, a rent-a-cop pulled him over. He informed the rent-a-cop that he (the rent-a-cop) had no authority. The rent-a-cop replied, "I am telling God on you." When my friend awoke from the dream, the Lord gave him the interpretation. The Lord said that he had placed me in the position of a rent-a-cop and did not acknowledge me as a woman of God who walked in the power of the Lord. The Lord went on to tell him that, "all of heaven backs her [me] up." I must admit that hearing the Lord's word concerning me was astonishing. It changed my friend's perspective of me. Because he now views me through the eyes of the Lord. To deny the power of God working in and through an individual is to deny the Word of God spoken directly to you. That, my dear reader is a dangerous thing and it places the blood directly on your hands.

When my friend came to me with his

acknowledgement of God's eye view, I must say that it gave confirmation to what I always knew. At the same time, it saddened me to realize that I was nothing in his eyes. Just a woman that supplied a need. Just a woman with no power or authority in the spirit realm. Just a woman operating a ministry in the basement of a bank building. Just a woman with no fire or anointing.

Just a woman...

We must be careful when we put labels on others. We must also be careful when we attempt to place a value on a person. It is also dangerous to place an individual on a pedestal simply because they tickle your ears, preach in a dynamic style or sing with a voice of an angel. The person you devalue might be the very person God wants to use to bless you. I pray you get that in your spirit.

The church has a habit of placing a high value on individuals who are flashy and always the life of the church party. While at the same time minimizing individuals who are gentle or soft spoken. The church often equates loud, boisterous dynamics or theatrics with power and anointing. The danger in this misconception is that we are denying the power of God flowing through individuals who are deemed quiet. The other side of that coin is that we might be giving the spirit of Jezebel or Tamar an open door.

Loud does not mean anointed. Just as charismatic does not mean powerful. The church must come to this realization; otherwise, we run the risk of being deceived. "Beware that your hearts are not deceived, and that you do not turn away and serve other gods and worship them" (Deuteronomy 11:16). "Do not be deceived, my beloved brethren. "Every good thing given and every perfect gift is from above, coming down from the Father of lights, with whom there is no variation or shifting shadow" (James 1:16-17).

We must place our faith in the power of the true and living God. We must stop looking at our co-laborers as less than who God created us to be. We must not allow the world, the church or individuals to devalue us simply because we are women. We must not continue to lower the bar in the church simply to satisfy and justify the status quo.

Have we lowered the standards of the church?

A Woman of Worth: Loving the Skin I'm In

Chapter 9

Has the Church Lowered the Bar?

The church has lowered its standards to the point that we accept almost anything in the pulpit. We must be very careful that the church does not become a modern day Antiochus Epiphanes and defile the temple of God. Antiochus demanded worship and established an image in the temple. As ministers of the Gospel, we must be careful not to steal God's glory by succumbing to the idea that the people worship us or believe that our image is the image people must see. In other words, we place our values or our worship in the

A Woman of Worth: Loving the Skin I'm In

wrong place.

I am making this comparison for one reason: the modern day church would rather have a backslidden, whore mongering, pimping from the pulpit man rather than a Holy Ghost filled, fire breathing, sold out woman. Why? Because the church has been brainwashed into believing that God is not calling women to ministry. A sad commentary to say the least. Without delving into a subject that would take volumes to resolve, let's look at Genesis 1:26-28: *"And God said, Let us make man in our image, after our likeness: and let them have dominion over the fish of the sea, and over the fowl of the air, and over the cattle, and over all the earth, and over every creeping thing that creepeth upon the earth. So God created man in his own image, in the image of God created he him; male and female created he them. And God blessed them, and God said unto them, Be fruitful, and multiply, and replenish the earth, and subdue it: and have dominion over the fish of the sea, and over the fowl of the air, and over every living thing that moveth upon the earth."*

God created male and female in His own image and they were to have dominion over the fish of the sea, and over the fowl of the air, and over the cattle, and over all the earth, and over every creeping thing that creeps upon the earth. God went on to bless them, and commanded them, to be fruitful, multiply, replenish and subdue the earth.

Every command God gave, he gave it to **them**. He did not give it to the man alone. He gave it to man and woman in order to accomplish a great work on the earth. When God gave the command to subdue the earth He was not gender specific. Meaning, He did not single out men and command them to subdue. God issued a command to co-laborers on the earth, Adam and Eve. He called Eve Adam's "helper" in Genesis 2:18. God said, "It is not good for the man to be alone. I will make a helper suitable for him."

God then caused the man to fall into a deep sleep; and while he was sleeping, he took one of the man's ribs and closed up the place with flesh. Then the LORD God made a woman from the rib he had taken out of the man, and he brought her to the man. The man said, "This is now bone of my bones and flesh of my flesh; she shall be called 'woman,' for she was taken out of man" (Genesis 2:21-23 paraphrased).

God created woman to be a helper. God also said; let ***"them"*** have dominion over the earth. Why is it that when it comes to the work of ministry, women are relegated to the back burner? Scriptures are often used to justify why women should not be allowed to minister in churches. The Word of God is also used to justify why women should not hold positions of authority.

The scripture most often cited comes from the words of the Apostle Paul when he wrote that women should keep silent in church. *"Let your women keep silence in the churches: for it is not permitted unto them to speak; but they are commanded to be under obedience, as also saith the law. And if they will learn any thing, let them ask their husbands at home: for it is a shame for women to speak in the church"* (1 Cor. 14:34-35).

At first glance, it might appear that the Apostle Paul is devaluing women in the Corinthian church. However, it is quite the opposite. In order to understand the Apostle Paul's reasoning, you must first understand the culture and the times.

Let the women keep silence in the churches. Obviously, this must be interpreted in light of 11:5 where it is clear that Paul understood that women were permitted to prophesy and to pray in public worship so long as they were properly dressed.[1]

And if they will learn any thing, let them ask their husbands at home. They were not allowed to disrupt the service by asking questions and talking while the service was going on.[2]

---

[1] Nelson KJV Bible Commentary, pp. 1494.
[2] Nelson KJV Bible Commentary, pp. 1494.

But every woman that prayeth or prophesieth with her head uncovered dishonoureth her head: for that is even all one as if she were shaven (1Cor. 11:5).

Prayeth or prophesieth with her head uncovered. A further teaching of this verse shows that women prophesied and prayed in public worship. This no doubt, involved edifying, exhorting, and comforting. Apparently, this did not constitute a point of contention, since the apostle does not feel obligated to speak directly to it. Yet this is not a contradiction to 1 Corinthians 13:34-37.[3]

Paul never demeaned women in his writings he was establishing order. Careful study of the

---

[3] Nelson KJV Bible Commentary, pp. 1484.

ministry of the Apostle Paul will show that he ministered with many women throughout his ministry and he also held them in high esteem. Women such as:

- I commend unto you **Phoebe** our sister, which is a servant of the church, which is at Cenchrea (Romans 16:1).

- Salute Andronicus and **Junia,** my kinsmen, and my fellow prisoners, who are of note among **the apostles** (Romans 16:7).

- Greet **Priscilla** and Aquila my helpers in Christ Jesus (Romans 16:3).

- Greet **Mary,** who bestowed much labour on us (Romans 16:6).

- Salute **Tryphena** and **Tryphosa**, who labour in the Lord (Romans 16:12).

- Salute the beloved **Persis**, which laboured much in the Lord (Romans 16:12).

- Salute Philologus, and **Julia**, Nereus, and **his sister**, and **Olympas**, and all the saints which are with them (Romans 16:15).

Women held a prominent place in Paul's life and ministry. Women were celebrated and not simply tolerated. They occupied various stations and all are represented as performing a valuable service for the Lord. The fact that he referred to Phoebe as a deaconess and to Junia as an apostle, is clear evidence that he saw nothing wrong or unusual in women having significant offices in the early church. Paul esteemed women highly for their work's sake and it is certainly wrong to label Paul, based on First Corinthians 14:34 and First Timothy 2:11-15, as a misogynist (hater of women).

As the modern day church, it would be wise to research and establish an understanding of the state of the women the Apostle Paul addressed in his letters. Paul addressed issues with women who were out of order in the church, and he found it necessary to establish order through his letters to the churches.

In a study entitled *Women in the Church: Biblical Data Report* (1997), the Dallas theological Seminary noted the following concerning women's relationships to the Holy Spirit:

- The Holy Spirit fell on men and women on the Day of Pentecost (Acts 2:1-4).
- The Holy Spirit used women as His prophetic mouthpiece (Philip's four daughters were prophetesses, Acts 21:8-9).

A Woman of Worth: Loving the Skin I'm In

- The Holy Spirit indwells women (Roman 8:9), and women's bodies also serve as a sanctuary of the Holy Spirit (1 Cor. 6:9-20).
- In Christ a woman is given the same spiritual gifts available to men today, including pasturing, teachings, and evangelism (1 Cor. 12:7-11; 27-31; Rom. 12:3-8; 1 Pet. 4:10, 11).
- Paul recognized that the Holy Spirit used women as His prophetic mouthpiece (1 Cor. 11:3).

The bible tells us in 2 Timothy 2:15: "Study and be eager and do your utmost to present yourself to God approved (tested by trial), a workman who has no cause to be ashamed, correctly analyzing and accurately dividing [rightly handling and skillfully teaching] the Word of Truth" (AMP). We must accurately divide the Word of Truth if we are to teach a subject as sensitive as the subject of women in ministry.

It's time to raise the bar and allow the people of God to flow in the areas of ministry God called them to and end the years of segregation that have plagued the church for centuries.

Chapter 10

Are You a Grasshopper In Your Own Eyes?

Recently, I was having lunch with an awesome woman of God who shared her experience of being devalued by the individuals around her. She spoke of how the people in her circle tried to demean the ministry God birthed in her. She spoke of how she complained to the Lord about their put downs and negative comments. During prayer the Lord asked, "Are you a grasshopper in your own eyes?" The Lord can ask questions that will cause you to stop in your tracks and reevaluate everything around you. He has a way of drawing your attention to the traps, snares and manipulations of the enemy.

Are you a grasshopper in your own eyes? Have you allowed society, family or friends to belittle you? Have you allowed the enemy to open old wounds that leave you doubting who you are? Have you allowed the enemy to devalue you and shut down the flow of God in your life?

> **Every woman has value, remember you are the apple of God's eye.**

There will be times when the people around you will not see the power of God working in your life. They will not see the value of what God is doing in your ministry, church or home. It will come from people close to you, individuals you would never believe viewed you in a devalued light. Jesus said to them, *"Only in his hometown and in his own house is a prophet without honor"* (Matthew 13:57). The Lord is telling us that among the people closest to you, you will be without honor or value.

Often the people around you don't intend to harm you, but they have become FAMILIAR with you and therefore, they don't see the marvelous work that you are to God. Another term that might be helpful - they become COMMON with you. To become COMMON means: without special privilege, rank, or status. In other words instead of referring to you as Pastor Kay, you are simply Kay. When we allow people to become "common" with us, they tend to devalue the calling on your life. I didn't say your title, office or position, I am speaking of your calling.

A Woman of Worth: Loving the Skin I'm In

We are not to be caught up in titles, positions or offices, but by the same measure, we should never allow anyone to devalue the call on our lives, the work that we perform or the choices we make.

Never allow anyone to make you feel like a grasshopper in your own eyes. Never allow them to make you feel small and insignificant. You are the apple of God's eye and therefore, to Him you are treasure beyond price.

We cannot change the mindset of people, but we don't have to buy into their misconceptions. Moreover, we don't have to allow their perspective of us to belittle us either. Love them, pray for them and **LIVE YOUR LIGHT BEFORE THEM.**

Every woman has value, remember you are the

A Woman of Worth: Loving the Skin I'm In

apple of God's eye. *Even Rehab had value...*

A Woman of Worth: Loving the Skin I'm In

Chapter 11

Even Rahab Had Value

"Then Joshua son of Nun secretly sent two spies from Shittim. "Go, look over the land," he said, "especially Jericho." So they went and entered the house of a prostitute named Rahab and stayed there. The king of Jericho was told, "Look! Some of the Israelites have come here tonight to spy out the land." So the king of Jericho sent this message to Rahab: "Bring out the men who came to you and entered your house, because they have come to spy out the whole land." But the woman had taken the two men and hidden them. She said, "Yes, the men came to me, but I did not know where they had come from" (Joshua 2:1-4). "The city and all that is in it are to be devoted to the LORD. Only Rahab the prostitute and all who are with her in her house shall be spared, because she hid the spies we sent" (Joshua 6:17).

Just as the prostitute, Rahab was valuable to the kingdom of God, it is important for you to know that you are valuable in the eyes of God. It does not matter what you are called to do in life, you are precious in the eyes of the Lord. Rahab was valuable to God's purpose for His people and He used her to do a great work that resulted in her entire family being spared death and destruction.

Your call may not be to the ministry field, but that does not lessen who you are and what you are called to do. If you are a bus driver, be the best driver you can. If you are a server, be the best server you can be. If you are a ditch digger, be the best. Whatever you do in life, do it for the glory of God. Your value is in WHOM YOU ARE not what you do. NEVER allow anyone to define you according to your social or economic status, job, title or any superficial label.

Rahab had a past, but that did not stop God from using her to do a great work. Never allow your past to keep you from the work God has for you. It is a great work and it may require using elements from your past to strengthen you for your future. Crawling around on the ground strengthens your knees, so use your strong knees in your prayer life.

You are the woman that God says you are and nothing and no one can change that. You are a woman of inheritance.

Chapter 12

A Woman of Inheritance

Then the daughters of Zelophehad, the son of Hepher, the son of Gilead, the son of Machir, the son of Manasseh, of the families of Manasseh the son of Joseph, came near; and these are the names of his daughters: Mahlah, Noah and Hoglah and Milcah and Tirzah. They stood before Moses and before Eleazar the priest and before the leaders and all the congregation, at the doorway of the tent of meeting, saying, "Our father died in the wilderness, yet he was not among the company of those who gathered themselves together against the LORD in the company of Korah; but he died in his own sin, and he had no sons. "Why should the name of our father be withdrawn from among his family because he had no son? Give us a possession among our father's brothers." So Moses brought their case before the LORD (Numbers 27:1-5).

The request was brought to Moses by the five daughters of Zelophehad, whose genealogy is traced back to Manasseh, concerned the securing of the inheritance and the preservation of their father's name in the land. Their action in approaching the leaders of the nation was unprecedented, a great act of courage, conviction, and faith. When the women made their claim to Moses, they specified that their father had not died because of participation in the rebellion of

Korah (see Numbers 16) but only because he was part of the entire doomed first generation.

This situation deals with the Law of Inheritance and the complicating factor of women who are inheritors of land and who might marry outside their families and thus muddle the subsequent inheritance claims of Israel.

We have an inheritance promised to us by the Lord. An inheritance that is worth more than money or gold. God does not want us to muddle our inheritance claims with fear, doubt, anger, negativity, unforgiveness, jealousy, envy or devaluation. Devaluation will cause you to SETTLE for less than God's best for you. It will stop the flow of God in your life and hinder your

inheritance transfer. Receiving our inheritance from the Lord will come when we refuse to accept the lies of the enemy and his spiritual assassins. Satan is not concerned with how he acquires your inheritance, his objective is to steal, kill and destroy it. Never allow the enemy to rob you of your inheritance.

A capable, intelligent, and virtuous woman—who is he who can find her? She is far more precious than jewels and her value is far above rubies or pearls (Proverbs 31:10). *You are a woman of worth and you are B.A.D.!*

Chapter 13

I'm BAD!

You are a mighty woman of God!
You are fearfully and wonderfully made.
You are BAD! Beautiful, Amazing and Destined.

We are not simply women; we are mighty women of God. We are fearfully and wonderfully made by God to do a great work for God.

We are BAD!

You are BAD! Beautiful, Amazing and Destined.

Unfortunately, when we are devalued we don't see the beauty and strength within us. I pray that the next paragraph stirs something within you to see the beauty that is inside of you.

It is important to know that you are a capable, intelligent, and virtuous woman. You comfort and encourage, as you strive to do only good in the lives of those around you. You are girded with strength; spiritual, mental, and physical, for your God-given tasks and your arms are strong and firm. Strength and dignity are your clothing and your position is strong and secure. You are a woman who reverently and worshipfully fears the Lord, and for that, you shall be praised!

> *You are a mighty woman of God!*
> *You are fearfully and wonderfully made.*
> *You are BAD! Beautiful, Amazing and*
> *Destined for the fullness of God.*

Sista! YOU ARE BAD! **Beautiful, amazing** and **destined** to great things in life. Never allow anyone or anything to take that away from you.

Know your strengths and weaknesses and work on them both. Don't leave open doors or gateways for the enemy to have access. There are awesome things in store for you, your requirement is to walk it out. Walk through the doors that God opens for you and don't look back at the doors He closes. Stand firm in your place in God and know without a doubt that you are a woman of purpose and destiny.

As you go through life with all its trials and tribulations, learn to love the skin you are in!

A Woman of Worth: Loving the Skin I'm In

Chapter 14

A Woman of Worth: Loving the Skin I'm In

I read an article by a female author where she describes herself. It was an encouragement to me and I tailored it to the woman that I am. I hope that you will take this same format and write a declaration of who you are. I believe it will encourage you to love the skin you're in because it will equip you to describe your view of YOU.

 **Rabbit trail**: There's journal space in the back to write out your declaration. Write it several times.

A Woman of Worth: Loving the Skin I'm In

The more you grow, the more it will change.

Jacquie: A Woman of Worth

I am an author, a teacher, a psalmist, a visionary. I approach the world with the eyes of an artist, the ears of a musician, the heart of a psalmist and the soul of a writer. I see rainbows where others see only rain and possibilities where others only see problems. I love spring flowers, a summer breeze, and the beauty of the leaves in the fall, and snow flakes gently falling on my face. I see the hand of God in the smallest of creatures and hear the voice of God in the still of the night. Classical music, eclectic art, and horseback riding are sources of inspiration, as well as jazz music, a cracking fireplace, and old movies. I love to write; words flow easily from my fingertips as my heart beats rapidly with excitement as an idea becomes a reality on the paper in front of me. I use all of these elements to encourage myself and the people around me. I'm a learner and a seeker of knowledge, and I take those with a desire to learn along on my journey. I smile often, and laugh easily, and I weep at pain and cruelty. I love what I do, and by the grace of God, I'm good at it. I learned to dream through reading, learned to create dreams through writing, and learned to develop dreamers through teaching. I shall always be a dreamer and a woman after God's own heart. *I am a woman of worth and loving the skin, I'm in.*

Mama J Got Her Spiritual Swagger Back

Recently, I attended the American Black Music Awards in Chicago, IL and received the Image

Award for worldwide evangelism. The event was wonderful and I enjoyed time with my family. When I arrived at MCI airport, I was walking through the terminal and I noticed that I had a little something extra in my step. I stopped, checked myself and asked, "What is that?" I giggled and replied, "Girl, you got a swagger." Now where did that come from? "Mama J, got her swagger back." I giggled again and continued walking.

When you walk through a place, where you have been devalued and suddenly find yourself in a new realm, sphere, level or dimension - a small voice inside of you gently says, "Girl you have come through the worst of it. You withstood the let downs, put-downs, shut downs and hand me downs. Now, God has given you a spiritual swagger that says, I AM BAD! I am

A Woman of Worth: Loving the Skin I'm In

BEAUTIFUL, AMAZING AND DESTINED for greatness. I am walking in the power of the Almighty, El Shaddai." When you get that in your spirit then you will have a reason to strut with confidence in the One who gave you the abilities, gifts and talents.

Walking through the airport and realizing who I am IN GOD and what I am worth TO GOD, meant more than any award, more than any accolade from man and more than money, fortune or fame. Knowing who you are and whose you are means EVERYTHING. The recognition in Chicago was fine and I appreciate the ABMA Association for considering me, but the recognition from the Lord is ALL I will ever need. I discovered my freedom in Him and His great love for me and I will never allow anyone to devalue my worth in God again.

A Woman of Worth: Loving the Skin I'm In

I am a woman of worth and I love the skin I'm in...

Chapter 15

Love Yourself in the Process

As you grow and go through life, you will encounter many trials, tribulations and obstacles. The most important fact you need to know is that you MUST love yourself in the process. We are the work of God's awesome hand and you are a work in progress. Change will come as you embrace every obstacle that is presented to you. Growth will come as you learn from them. Your passion is tied to the things you deem valuable and your purpose will grow through them.

Step up to each door with a holy determination that when the door opens up to you, you will walk through it, without fear or doubt. There will be days when doubt tries to rear it's ugly head, but know that you are more than a conqueror and you are an over comer. You are a mighty woman of God, capable of pulling down strongholds and casting down every imagination that exalts itself against what you know to be true based on the promises and word of God.

Therefore, stand on the promises and the word of God. Stand girded up in your heart, mind and spirit knowing that God is bringing a great victory to your life.

It does not matter what the people around you say, what matters is what God says. Matthew 10:1 tells us that Jesus gave us authority over unclean spirits, to cast them out, and to heal every kind of disease and every kind of sickness.

A Woman of Worth: Loving the Skin I'm In

As a mighty woman you have the authority, **use it**. God is calling you to be confident in Him so that when He opens doors and platforms you are ready. There will be people that see you as arrogant and bossy, but in the spirit realm, God is calling it authority. Some will call you controlling or overbearing, but God is calling it authority, ability and power. Walk in your place of authority in humility, submission and obedience and God will do the rest.

You are a woman of worth, worthy to be celebrated and not tolerated. If you find yourself in a place where people are tolerating you, GET OUT! Their toleration will lead to your subjugation (defeat, overthrow, conquest) to the voice of the enemy.

Stand on the promises of God for your life.

Believe that God has great plans for you. Again, it does not matter where you are today, what matters are where you are going and how you will get there. Take the journey of discovery and learn from every step because you will be able to help other sisters along the way.

Chapter 16

Discovering the Butterfly in You

I like to think of myself as a butterfly because of the life changing metamorphosis of a butterfly. A butterfly starts out as a caterpillar, which is a young insect or worm with a long soft body, many short legs, and often brightly colored or spiny skin. It crawls along making his way through life. The caterpillar's due season arrives and it is time to begin the journey of becoming the beautiful new creature God created him to be.

A Woman of Worth: Loving the Skin I'm In

The caterpillar begins spinning a cocoon (*the silky covering with which a caterpillar or other insect larva encloses itself during its transition to an adult state*) in which to enclose himself or to hide himself from the world. As the caterpillar is suspended within the cocoon, changes are occurring that will birth out a new creature very unrecognizable to the world. Chemical adjustments are made to his DNA, bodily functions change, even the thought process begins to change. I believe that the mind of the caterpillar must be renewed if he is going to function to the fullest of his potential. Otherwise, the new butterfly would be crawling around on the ground trying to find his destiny.

Once the caterpillar has been hidden in the cocoon for the designated period, his due season arrives and he begins the ardent task of being birthed out of the cocoon. Slowly the cocoon releases the new creation to the world. A new creature emerges from the cocoon ready to greet the world and begin his new life.

> **Talitha Cumi means *Daughter ARISE*! Arise woman of purpose and destiny and take your rightful place as a WOMAN OF PASSION and a WOMAN OF PURPOSE, a WOMAN OF WORTH.**

Although his process is not complete, he knows that a change has occurred. Because of the new mindset, the caterpillar instinctively knows that there is still work to be done in and through him if he is going to receive all that God has for him.

He then finds a place in which to allow the sun to dry his wings and strengthen his heart for his new journey. He sits perched as the sun prepares him for his new season in life. Once his wings are dry and blood has filled them properly, the butterfly is now ready to fly.

The new creation emerges with beauty and splendor. With strong wings, the butterfly can soar to the highest heights. The destiny before him is great because he can fly to the places the caterpillar only dreams of. The butterfly is the ultimate idea of man's transformation in the spirit.

Imagine you are a caterpillar, crawling your way out of suicidal thoughts, drugs, alcohol, sexual promiscuity, sexual abuse, spousal abuse, depression, un-forgiveness, fear, doubt, unbelief or another of Satan's evil traps. Before we surrendered our lives to Christ, we were like the caterpillar, crawling around trying to find our way. After we surrendered to the Lord, He began to spin a spiritual cocoon in which to hide us from the hand of the enemy so He could do a work in us. He began to change our spiritual DNA to reflect His DNA in mind, heart and spirit. He filled us with His Word and showed us His great love and tender care. He protected us from the hand of the enemy as he began to mold us into the beautiful image He pre-destined for us. While we were in the cocoon, he changed our mindset so that we could begin to walk in the fullness of life. He changed our heart so that it is strong and sure. He placed within us a desire to soar for the Kingdom of God. He purged out old habits and desires that caused us to crawl through life settling for less than His best.

Once the process was complete, we emerged from our spiritual cocoon a new creature in

Christ Jesus. However, He was not finished with us. He then placed us on a windowsill in order to allow the "SON" to dry our spiritual wings and strengthen our hearts to go the distance in life. He did not want us to come off the sill too soon because wet wings could mean disaster. A weak heart could mean we fall prey to the devices of the enemy. In other words, if we come off the sill too soon we could do more harm to ourselves and fail to reach our fullest potential. Too many believers get in a hurry, leave the sill or shelf before they are ready, and miss being "dried" or "tried" by the Lord.

The Lord once told me, *"I am taking my time with you so that you do not fall prey to pride and greed and fail."* After seeing so many powerful men and women of God fall prey to the bait of Satan through sexual immorality, greed, perversions, drugs and the like - I understand completely and I am grateful that the Lord loves me so much that He did not allow me to move off the shelf too soon. He kept me hidden until he time came when He knew that my wings were strong and my heart was sure in Him. The Lord needs strong men and women who will stand in the midst of the battle and not fall prey to the snares of the enemy. We will have a foundation that is built firmly on the Word and promises of God. Therefore, the snares of devaluation, insecurity, inferiority and others like it won't be a hindrance to our destiny in God.

We will hunger and thirst for the things that give Him glory. We will hunger for more of Him. When God is in your future - all limits are off. When the limits, bondages and snares are stripped away, all that is left is YOU and GOD.

A Woman of Worth: Loving the Skin I'm In

You are a beautiful butterfly, free of the limitations that have held you captive. You are no longer a caterpillar so stop crawling around settling for less than God's best for you. It is time to fly like the butterfly God created you to be. Talitha Cumi means *Daughter ARISE*! Arise woman of purpose and destiny and take your rightful place as a WOMAN OF PASSION and a WOMAN OF PURPOSE, a WOMAN OF WORTH.

I pray that my journey of discovery has helped you come into the knowledge of who you are and whose you are. You are a woman of worth and it's time that you love the skin you are in. Be blessed.

(Discovering the butterfly in You was taken from my book entitled: Trapped in the Arms of Death: Overcoming the Grip of Suicide)

Remember, you are B.A.D.

Beautiful

Amazing &

Destined

A Woman of Worth: Loving the Skin I'm In

About the Author

God has called Jacquie Hadnot to encourage, inspire, motivate and activate the gifts of the Spirit in order to raise powerful ministries in the body of Christ. She is becoming a voice on the subject of prayer, worship and spiritual warfare.

She is recognized as a modern-day apostle with a strong prophetic and psalmist anointing. She has a revelational teaching ministry with a mandate to saturate the world with the Word of God. Jacquie's heart is to see people arise and walk in the destiny and inheritance of the Lord.

She has founded and established It Is Written Ministries, a publication company, an accounting and consulting firm, and a global radio station.

A Woman of Worth: Loving the Skin I'm In

As a retired accountant and financial executive, Jacquie blends ministerial and entrepreneurial applications in her ministry to enrich and empower a diverse audience with skills and abilities to take kingdoms for the Lord Jesus Christ. A lecturer, conference speaker, teacher, business trainer, and financial consultant, she provides consulting services to businesses, churches, and individuals. She has written over twenty-five books, manuals, and other materials on intimacy with God, prayer, fasting and spiritual warfare. She has also released several music Cds and received numerous music and book publishing awards.

Beyond the pulpit, Jacquie is a talk-show host on both television and radio with her own program, Light for Your Path. Weekly she applies God's wisdom to today's world solutions. Her ministry goal is to make Christ's teachings relevant for today. She also publishes a quarterly magazine by the same name.

In addition to her vast experience, Jacquie has a Th.d. in Pastoral Theology and a Masters in Ministry Leadership. She is also a wife, mother of one daughter and grandmother of one grandson. She and her husband, Gregory presently pastor It Is Written Ministries in Kansas City Kansas. They also serve as owners and officers of Igniting the Fire Media Group.

A Woman of Worth: Loving the Skin I'm In

Other Books & Materials by Dr. Jacquie

Books in Print

- The Art of Spiritual Warfare: Strategies for Effective Warfare
- There's A Famine in the Land: *Overcoming Great Recession*
- Your Declaration of Dependence on God
- Closing the Doors to Satan's Attacks: *Overcoming Fear*
- Trapped in the Arms of Death: *Overcoming Grip of Suicide*
- The Extravagant Love of God: Experiencing the Prophetic Flow
- Cry Aloud, Spare Not! A Prophetic Call to Fast God Has Chosen
- Cry Aloud, Spare Not! The Companion-Study Guide
- His Mercy Endures Forever: Psalms, Prayers & Meditations
- To Make War with the Saints; Satan's Kingdom Agenda
- A Treasure in the Pleasure of Loving God
- Loving God through His Names: 365 Days of the Year
- Where Is Your God? Have We Lost Referential Fear of the Lord?

Booklets

- When Fear Crept In
- Deeper...
- Naked, Broken and Unashamed

A Woman of Worth: Loving the Skin I'm In

Audio Books & Teachings
- More of You… (Volume 1)
- In the Face of Adversity: *Overcoming Life's Storms*
- Be Not Deceived…
- Where Is Your God?
- Recognizing Your Due Season
- Praying the Healing Scriptures
- The Enemy in Me: *Overcoming Self-Life Issues*
- Trusting God in a Season of Discouragement
- The Harlot Heart

Music
- The Extravagant Love of God
- The Spoken Word of Love
- His Mercy Endures Forever: Praying the Psalms

DVD
- When Your Faith is Being Tested
- What Made David Run
- Agents of Change
- Virtuous Women of Worship

TO CONTACT DR. JACQUIE:
www.jacquiehadnot.com
www.ignitingthefire.net
Or write us:
jacquie@jacquiehadnot.com

A Woman of Worth: Loving the Skin I'm In
Also available

A Woman of Worth Study Guide
A comprehensive study guide designed to reinforce the teachings from the book and the conference.

A Woman of Worth Journal
To help you on your journey of discovering the woman God pre-destined you to become. Journaling is a great way to keep your thoughts and meditations on paper.

Coming Soon!
A Woman of Worth Audio Book
A Woman of Worth E-Book

You are a woman of worth

A Woman of Worth: Loving the Skin I'm In

You are a woman of worth

A Woman of Worth: Loving the Skin I'm In

You are a woman of worth

A Woman of Worth: Loving the Skin I'm In

You are a woman of worth

You are a woman of worth

www.ingramcontent.com/pod-product-compliance
Lightning Source LLC
Chambersburg PA
CBHW071123090426
42736CB00012B/1993